the organised mum method

JOURNAL

Sort Your Life Out One Day at a Time

GEMMA BRAY

PIATKUS

Also by Gemma Bray

The Organised Mum Method

The Organised Time Technique

Gemma Bray started The Organised Mum Method in 2006 when her first child was born. Fed up with the housework getting out of control, she devised a cleaning routine and stuck it on the fridge. TOMM was born. In January 2017, Gemma put it all down in a blog and shared TOMM with readers. The response was a phenomenon, with TOMM devotees crediting the method with transforming their home life. The book, *The Organised Mum Method,* followed in 2019 and quickly became a *Sunday Times* bestseller.

Having shown us how to master housework to stop it taking over our lives, a year later Gemma wrote *The Organised Time Technique*, a method for taking control of the rest of your day so that you can spend your time on the things that are most important to you. In this book, Gemma distils those two methods into a format that will help you take back control of your time and how you spend it.

PIATKUS

First published in Great Britain in 2021 by Piatkus

3 5 7 9 10 8 6 4 2

A CIP catalogue record for this book is available from
the British Library.

ISBN 978-0-349-42950-2

Typeset by EM&EN
Printed and bound in Great Britain by Clays Ltd, Elcograf S.p.A

Papers used by Piatkus are from well-managed forests
and other responsible sources.

PIATKUS
An imprint of
Little, Brown Book Group
Carmelite House
50 Victoria Embankment
London EC4Y 0DZ

An Hachette UK Company
www.hachette.co.uk

Contents

INTRODUCTION – DON'T SKIP THIS, IT'S IMPORTANT!

I know that you will be raring to get going; I mean, who doesn't love a fresh, clean, shiny journal? You can almost *smell* the possibilities. But, before you jump in, there is some brief housekeeping that we need to cover. I want to explain how this book came to be and how you can get the most out of it. You see, this isn't just any old journal. It is the culmination of years of work; of talking to families, new parents, single parents, people who feel overwhelmed and people who are searching for a way to bring some order to their lives.

This is my third book. The first, *The Organised Mum Method: Transform your home in 30 minutes a day*, was written to help exhausted parents tackle the housework; while my second, *The Organised Time Technique: How to get your life running like clockwork*, was designed to help people take charge of the rest. This journal integrates those two methods, giving you a practical way to structure your time, and put everything that you have learnt into practice. It will help you to plan and prep so that you'll be able fit in the stuff you really want to do. Not read the first two books? Don't worry, I will guide you through the main principles in the coming pages so that you can get going as quickly as possible.

My books exist to make people's lives easier. I wish I had them back when I had my first baby. Since that time, I have had to learn a lot about how to be organised. I created the methods and techniques that I share in my books out of necessity – back then they stopped me from losing myself in the daily grind.

It all started when I was a new mum, over 15 years ago. Things were slightly different then. For one, social media wasn't really a thing – well, it was, but it was only really Facebook and MySpace. Instagram and TikTok were just a twinkle in their developers' eyes. Although things weren't as technologically fancy as they are now, the fundamentals of life as a new mum were still pretty much the same as they are today.

I faced the same highs and lows as many new mums. I was perplexed about afterpains, I struggled with breastfeeding and I simply couldn't believe the whole new level of tiredness caused by the sleep deprivation of having a newborn. I had spent my entire pregnancy prepping for what I thought motherhood was going to be like. But we all know the saying 'man plans, God laughs', or, in my case, 'woman plans, God gives her stretchmarks'.

Becoming a parent is life-changing and even if you have more than one child already and think you've nailed it, you soon discover that every child and every pregnancy is different. It can feel like one hell of a roller-coaster. Thankfully, as with any good roller-coaster there are some amazing highs to counteract the lows and that, at the end of the day, is what makes parenthood so rewarding. Sometimes, though, the struggles can seem hard to fight through.

I had one such struggle with my first baby. I had planned for what I imagined it would be like, but the reality was something very different. When I left my house to go to the hospital to give birth, it was in pristine condition; the burping cloths were folded, the kitchen was clean and the crib was made up with crisp, white sheets. I was ready to be a mum.

The difference in the state of my house – and my mind – a week later was like night and day. My home looked like Primark on the first day of the sales.

I couldn't fathom how such a small human could wreak so much havoc. It felt like my whole life had been turned upside down. Not only did I feel an immense sense of responsibility for this gorgeous little boy who had chosen me to be his mum, but I still had to do all the other 'life' stuff that I was doing before, like the housework, the cooking, the shopping (oh and earn a living!). I clearly remember feeling as though I was in a bubble, as if there was a distance between me and the rest of the world. The real world felt a little bit out of reach and almost muffled. I remember watching the window cleaner doing his round as I was feeding Tom and wondering how the rest of the world could carry on as normal while I was going through one of the most transformative periods of my life.

The bubble of my babymoon burst eventually, and I emerged into the real world again. The visitors had gone, the congratulatory flower bouquets had long wilted and I was back to real life and all that came with it.

And what came with it was a massive dose of anxiety and a feeling that I simply wasn't coping. I struggled silently, berating myself for not living up to the expectations that I had set myself when I was pregnant. It wasn't playing out as I had hoped it would, so I set about controlling the only thing I could control – the cleaning. My rationale was if the house looked great then people would automatically assume that I had everything under control. But the cleaning began to take up more and more time until it reached the point where I was prioritising it above seeing friends and family. I hid behind the armour of my clean house and kept quiet about my inner struggles.

Luckily, with the help of a lovely health visitor, I was able to recognise the unhealthy pattern that I was in and began searching for a better way. The result? After long hours sitting at my kitchen table, pencil in hand, I created The Organised Mum Method (or TOMM, as it became affectionately known). And I have never looked back. Out of TOMM grew The Organised Time Technique (or, you guessed it, TOTT). Soon I had a whole system that could keep the wheels of my life turning, without feeling that I was about to be over-whelmed. I was able to keep all the boring 'life-admin' jobs under control, leaving me time for myself and to enjoy being with my children.

TOMM and TOTT were my own personal life rafts that I clung to, to get me through many a choppy period in my life – divorce and single parenthood being by far the trickiest.

I did, in the end, start to catch up with the world of social media and in 2016 I started to talk about my methods and techniques online. If you are a member of our online community, you will know what happened next. We now have hundreds of thousands of people all over the world following along and I couldn't be prouder to be able to help so many people calm the chaos.

It is the very same online community that has helped bring this journal to life. You have been asking me to produce it for so long and, at long last, here it is! I hope you love it. I have taken your suggestions and woven them into this practical journal. Look at it as your talisman against overwhelm and procrastination.

Whether you are already a dedicated TOMMer or you are new to my method, this journal has the power to get your life on track. It will help you get to grips with your never-ending to-do list, set up healthy habits and fulfil your goals and ambitions.

That's a lot of a power for a book! I hope that it will become your daily companion, keeping you on the straight and narrow, making sure that when you climb into bed at night you feel calm and happy.

Ready to start? Let's sort out your life one day at a time.

PART ONE

GETTING STARTED

HOW THE ORGANISED MUM METHOD (TOMM) WORKS

This section is for those of you who have not read my first book, *The Organised Mum Method: Transform your home in 30 minutes a day*, as well as those who need a refresher. It will help you to understand how my hugely popular house-keeping method works and how you can use it alongside this journal to help keep the household chores under control. You are going to love it. It's simple but oh so effective.

The Organised Mum Method operates on an 8-week cycle and for each week of TOMM that you complete, your house will get cleaner. There will no longer be any need for mammoth cleaning sessions and your home will always be 'surprise visitor' ready. If that sounds a bit ambitious or intim-idating, let me share a favourite TeamTOMM motto: good enough is good enough – we aim for progress not perfection. Keep this in mind as you read this section.

When I became a new mum, I started to over-clean. At the time I thought I had to appear to be some sort of supermum. I would clean for hours, but I would fixate on the same things. For me, it was the vacuuming (we had a black Labrador who would shed *a lot*, which probably explains my reasoning) and my cushions – they had to be arranged just so, *all the time*. This meant that there were some jobs that I would miss out completely, so while my house was immaculate in some areas, in others there was a build-up of dust and dirt. I did not have a system and that meant I was cleaning haphazardly. Little wonder then that I got despondent when I discovered an area of my home that I had neglected for a while. Feeling like I had failed, I would clean some more and so it went on.

When I created TOMM I knew that I needed an efficient and realistic way to keep on top of things. I needed a plan that would reassure me that things were going to get done: so, for instance, if I saw that the hallway was a little bit dusty at the end of a long day, I would be safe in the knowledge that it was hallway day soon and it could wait until then. This meant that I was able to down tools knowing that I had everything in hand. TOMM was born and after a few short weeks I found that I was cleaning less, *and* my house was cleaner than ever before.

What is this sorcery, I hear you ask ...

THE BASICS OF TOMM

Before we get on to the basics, it is important to be aware of one of the most vital principles that underpin TOMM: there is more to life than housework. For this reason, we don't clean at the weekend. On TeamTOMM we like to keep the weekends free for the fun stuff, like spending time with family and friends, pursuing hobbies or starting new ones.

Now let's put TOMM into action so we can enjoy all those free weekends. Here's how it works. TOMM is split into three levels of cleaning. Each is important in its own right but put them together and they make up one hell of an effective cleaning method. The levels are:

Level 1 Daily light-touch jobs that you do throughout the day

Level 2 A 30-minute routine of tasks that you carry out four days a week

Level 3 The Focus Day

Let's look at each of these in turn.

Level 1

These are the things most of us do on a daily basis, so the chances are you've already got much of this covered. I'm talking here about those basic jobs such as doing the washing-up, making the beds and so on. But you need to do these efficiently – and consistently – so that they only take you approximately 15 minutes each day, Monday to Friday. You can do them at the weekend if you want to – and a few of them, such as keeping on top of the kitchen, you probably will want to – but this is entirely optional. On page 12 you will find a list of your Level 1 jobs.

DAILY LEVEL 1 JOBS

✓ Quick floor clean of main living areas. This obviously depends on what floors you have (carpets, tiles, or wood floors). If you have hard flooring, mop it at least once a week.

✓ One load of laundry.

✓ Quick clean of bathrooms: this includes a mop of the floors at least once a week.*

✓ Make the beds.

✓ Keep on top of the kitchen as you go through the day.

*   Bathrooms are included in your Level 1 jobs, but you don't have to do the same thing every day. Make sure you change it up so that all areas of the bathroom are getting attention. So, for example, one day you might tackle the floors and another day you might do the mirror and sink (I do clean the toilet daily though).

When you dive into the journal you will see that there is a blank box in the Level 1 section. This is because we all have different lifestyles and homes. For example, I feed my chickens and collect their eggs as part of my Level 1s but you might want to add in walking the dog or making the kids' packed lunches for the next day. Use this blank box to customise your Level 1s as necessary.

Level 2 jobs

These make up the 30 minutes of cleaning that you do, over and above your Level 1 jobs, on four days of the week. I do Monday to Thursday and stick to same 30-minute routine each day, focusing on one particular room. Here's how I roll with that:

Monday: living room

Tuesday: bedrooms (affectionately nicknamed #cleansheettuesday)

Wednesday: hall and stairs

Thursday: kitchen

The checklist chart overleaf shows the Level 2 jobs that I include in that routine. A lot of people copy my TOMM routine – doing their living room on a Monday, bedrooms on a Tuesday and so on – but you can change the days on which you do particular rooms if you wish. Obviously, I can't tell you exactly what you need to do in your kitchen or living room, but my list gives you an idea of the tasks that apply to most people's homes. On page 38 you'll find a blank Level 2 checklist chart where you can list the tasks you want to include in your routine. Once you've decided what you will do, you should stick with your routine so that you get to know your TOMM days, and your tasks, off by heart. *Only spend 30 minutes a day on your Level 2 jobs.* That time limit will help you to focus and get things done efficiently. You won't have the time to sit and procrastinate.

GEMMA'S LEVEL 2 CHECKLIST

Monday: living room

- ✓ Tidy away anything that doesn't belong
- ✓ Wash throws and pet bedding
- ✓ A quick window clean, get rid of finger marks
- ✓ Sofa dive (vacuum under cushions)
- ✓ Dust
- ✓ Vacuum
- ✓ Mop if you have hard floors

Tuesday: bedrooms

- ✓ Strip beds
- ✓ Tidy away anything that doesn't belong
- ✓ Quick mine-sweep under beds
- ✓ Dust
- ✓ Vacuum
- ✓ Remake beds

Wednesday: hall and stairs

- ✓ Tidy away anything that doesn't belong
- ✓ Dust
- ✓ Vacuum
- ✓ Mop if you have hard floors

Thursday: kitchen	
✔ Empty the crumbs out of the toaster	✔ Clean the hob top
✔ Clean the inside of the microwave	✔ Give the sink a really good scrub
✔ Clean out the cutlery drawer(s)	✔ Wipe down all the working surfaces
✔ Quick fridge clean	✔ Wipe down the cupboard fronts
✔ Dust the blinds	✔ Vacuum and mop
✔ Clean the windows	
✔ Clean the splash-back behind the hob	

Focus Day

Each Friday I focus on a different room or area of the home. I call it my Friday Focus but, irrespective of the day you choose, having a Focus Day routine and sticking to it is the cornerstone of TOMM. It is the key to the whole shebang because it guarantees that the main areas of your home get a deep clean on a regular basis. On Focus Days you will still only clean for 30 minutes but, because you will already have been in that room very recently, you will be able to get down to the nitty-gritty straight away, without having to do a top-level tidy first. Even if you haven't got all the jobs done, you *must* down tools and put a full stop on your cleaning after

30 minutes. I promise you, if you are diligent and consistent, you will be doing enough cleaning. Remember what I said was one of the guiding principles of TOMM? That's right! Good enough is good enough.

There are 8 Focus Days days in total, which is why TOMM runs on an 8-week cycle:

Week 1: kids' bedrooms

Week 2: living room

Week 3: kitchen

Week 4: bathrooms

Week 5: main bedroom

Week 6: hall and stairs

Week 7: room of your choice

Week 8: garden/outside space

Opposite you'll find my Focus Day checklist to give you some ideas. (Again, in the 'How to make this journal work for you' section, you can fill out your own checklist if you wish, so that you can refer back to that until you get into the swing of things.)

Remember, the weekly Focus Day is the key to TOMM. It is your secret weapon to make sure that your home will keep on getting cleaner the longer you follow the plan. Don't skip it! I choose to do a Friday Focus, but if that doesn't work for you, do it on a day that suits you better.

GEMMA'S FOCUS DAY CHECKLIST

Remember: 30 minutes only!

Week 1: the kids' bedrooms

✓ Toy cull
✓ Cull clothes that no longer fit
✓ Straighten shelves/ bookcases

✓ Clean windows and mirrors
✓ Dust skirting boards
✓ Vacuum under furniture

Week 2: living room

✓ Shampoo rugs
✓ Clean cushion covers
✓ Clean sofa covers if they are removable

✓ Dust skirting boards
✓ Vacuum under furniture

Week 3: kitchen

✓ Pick two or three cupboards to declutter
✓ Clean extractor fan filters

✓ Clean the oven
✓ Clean the kickboards

Week 4: bathrooms

✓ Tackle the limescale
✓ Clean out the bathroom cabinet

✓ Tackle the grout
✓ Clean the windows
✓ Deep-clean the floors

Week 5: main bedroom

✓ Quick clothes/make-up cull
✓ Clean windows and mirrors

✓ Dust the skirting boards
✓ Vacuum under furniture

Week 6: hall and stairs

✓ Have a shoe/coat cull
✓ Go through lurking piles of paper
✓ Clean the banisters

✓ Clean the windows and mirrors
✓ Dust the skirting boards
✓ Vacuum under furniture
✓ Shampoo the rugs

Week 7: room of your choice

✓ Tidy away anything that does not belong/declutter
✓ Clean the windows and mirrors

✓ Dust the skirting boards
✓ Vacuum under furniture

Week 8: garden/outside space

✓ Clean the front door/doorstep
✓ Plant some seasonal flowers in pots

✓ Quick weed of flowerbed
✓ Sweep the patio
✓ Clean out the bin store

Remember: the Focus Day is the key to TOMM.

I realise there's a lot of information to absorb here and you're probably wondering how it all translates into the journal. On the following two pages you can see how I use it. This completed example is from Friday evening on Week 1 of the month. These checklists give me a bird's eye view of what still needs to get done in the house and what I have done (it's a Friday so, hey, all my cleaning tasks are completed and ticked!).

Of course, running a home isn't just about cleaning – we all need to eat. Planning our meals and food shopping also places demands on our time, which is why I like to record my meal plan for the week ahead and my shopping list alongside my cleaning tasks so that I have it all in one place.

Don't worry if you want to tweak things to suit your own home and lifestyle. That's the purpose of the 'How to make this journal work for you' section on page 35.

And if you are worried that 30 minutes a day does not seem enough, remember that the jobs suggested in my checklists are just that, suggestions – you can swap days, change and prioritise jobs depending on the type of house you live in and the type of lifestyle that you lead.

If you've got to this point and are thinking 'this is all very well but my house is a disaster zone and 30 minutes for the next two months won't scratch the surface', then head to 'The Clutter Buster' and 'The Messy House Bootcamp' in Part Three, which will help you have a good clear out or a housework reset before you start. If you feel as though you need a clean start (pun intended) this is a great place to begin.

MENU PLAN

MON
salmon & potato wedges
& peas

TUE
slow-cooker spag bol

WED
slow chilli & jackets

THURS
veg something-from-
nothing tart & salad

FRI
no cooking (leftovers)

SAT
Thai prawn curry & rice

SUN
slow-cooker lamb & veg

SHOPPING LIST

DAIRY
milk
cheddar cheese

PROTEIN
salmon
mince x 2
prawns
lamb shoulder

GROCERIES
rice
tomato puree
pasta

FRUIT & VEG
potatoes x 2
salad
green veg
red onions
apples

MY HOME — WEEK 1

DAILY JOBS

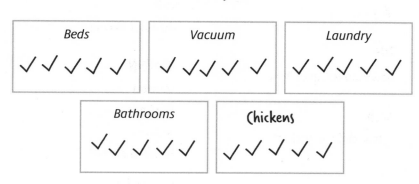

Beds	Vacuum	Laundry
✓✓✓✓✓	✓✓✓✓✓	✓✓✓✓✓

Bathrooms	Chickens
✓✓✓✓✓	✓✓✓✓✓

MONDAY TO FRIDAY

Living Room	Bedrooms	Hall and Stairs
✓	✓	✓

Kitchen
✓

Focus this Week

Kids' rooms
✓

THE ORGANISED TIME TECHNIQUE (TOTT) EXPLAINED

There's more to life than an organised home so, while TOMM sorts out your house, TOTT takes it further and sorts out the rest of your day. For those of you who aren't familiar with TOTT, or if you want a quick recap, here's how it came about.

TOTT morphed out of TOMM when I became a single mum. I was heartbroken and struggling to get through the days. But I couldn't press pause. I had to get Tom ready for school, change Jonny's nappy, make sure they were both well fed and loved. I had to work out how to cope financially, sell a house, find a new house, run a business … all while trying to not fall apart inside.

To help get my life back on track, I used to set my timer for 30 minutes and make myself do something productive. This ranged from powering through the jobs that I was putting off, such as working through my finances or phoning the solicitor to finalise my divorce, to going for a walk to clear my head. These small chunks of effort didn't overwhelm me, and I was able to get a lot done without it impacting on my already fragile state of mind. In short, I was sorting out my life, 30 minutes at a time.

It worked, so I've stuck with it. Over the years I've added to it and tweaked it, and it has morphed into a whole lifestyle technique that gets all the boring stuff done fast, so that I can spend as much time as possible doing the things that I enjoy.

TOTT is structured in a very similar way to TOMM – hey, if it isn't broke don't fix it – and splits our activities into three levels.

Level 1 – These are the foundations of your day. The things that MUST get done. Like eating and sleeping.

Level 2 – These things are not as important as Level 1 but still need to get done, such as work, the food shop, walking the dog and the housework.

Level 3 – These are the fun things that make you smile – hobbies, a relaxing bath, free time . . .

The whole point of TOTT is to make time for you to do the things you enjoy, because they are very important. If the thought of finding time for yourself seems completely unrealistic, don't worry, you are not going to get lost in the mundanity of life any more. This journal is going to help you to focus on yourself again.

PUTTING TOTT TOGETHER

TOTT frees you from having to constantly keep a mental tally of all the balls you are trying to juggle. This is achieved by splitting your days into time units, adding up the amount of time taken up with things that must get done and then deciding what you will do with the remaining time. I use 30-minute units, which means that I have 48 units each day to play with. By compartmentalising my time in this way (just as I do with TOMM), I can stay as focused as possible and keep procrastination at bay. Let me explain in more detail.

Before you can start planning your Level 3 'just for me' time, you need to know how much time you have available after you have done all the boring stuff that comes with being an adult. It would be easy to simply take a guesstimate, but this will do you no favours. You need to work with facts. If you've read *The Organised Time Technique* then you will have gone through the Time Bootcamp and will have a good idea how this works, but for newbies to TOTT and those who want a recap, here's a quick and easy way to work it out:

• Start with your Level 1 jobs, the non-negotiables. Work out how long these take you and assign time units to them.

• Next head to your Level 2 jobs. Do some maths and work out how many time units these will take up.

• Add your Level 1 to your Level 2 jobs. This is the amount of time that you need to commit to before you can see how much time you have left over for your Level 3 'me' time.

Level 1 units + Level 2 units = your time commitments

48 units (the amount of 30-minute units we all have in one day) – your time commitments = the number of free units you have available for Level 3 'me' time

It is totally normal at this point to either realise that you have no idea where all your time goes (social-media scroll hole, anyone?) or to come to the conclusion that you are over-committed and you don't have a single spare minute in the day to have a wee in peace, let alone have a long luxurious bath!

If you find yourself in the latter situation then you must act because all work and no play make for a very dull life indeed. Remember The Clutter Buster for your home that I referenced earlier? It is time to declutter your life! You need to be ruthless because something crucial is at stake: your 'me' time – your night out with friends or that cup of tea and a good book curled up in front of the fire.

When you can see in black and white what you have to work with, your Level 3 activities become completely guilt-free, because you know that you have either taken care of – or have made sure you have left enough time for – all of the other stuff that needs to get done (your Level 1s and Level 2s).

Think of it all fitting together a bit like the construction of a house. Your Level 1s are the foundations and walls, the important bits that hold up the rest of your life. The Level 2s are rooms and the doors and the Level 3s are the bits that make your house your home, the bits that make it uniquely yours, such as your art and your furniture.

BEING YOUR FUTURE FRIEND

The phrase 'future friend' has earned quite a reputation in TeamTOMM. Essentially, being your future friend means not putting off until tomorrow what you can do today. The idea is that whenever you don't want to do something – whether it applies to your job, your diet and fitness regime or your finances – you ask yourself, 'Am I making my life harder in the future? Am I being my future friend?' That future might be in an hour, a week or in a few months, but if the answer is yes, that your life is in some way going to be made worse by not doing it, then take a deep breath, be your future friend and get it ticked off your list. Do try it – I guarantee you'll be muttering this little phrase to yourself in all sorts of situations. You'll see that there's a space on the opening page of each month in the journal in Part Two for you to add any major future friend tasks that you need to tackle in the weeks ahead.

Overleaf you can see what a Monday to Friday in my life looks like. This is an example of my routine during a typical week in term time. As you can see, I have filled in the Level 1 and Level 2 activities so that I can clearly see the time I have remaining for Level 3s.

In the 'How to make this journal work for you' section there is a blank version of this time schedule diary for you to fill in. I realise that not everyone will want to be this prescriptive, but it really does help to see the framework of your week so that you have a good view of the time that is left for your lovely Level 3 'me' time stuff.

TIME	MONDAY	TUESDAY	WEDNESDAY
6	get ready	get ready	get ready
7	breakfast	breakfast	breakfast
8	school run	ToMM life admin	ToMM life admin
9			
10	work	work	work
11			
12			
1	work	work	work
2			
3	school run		school run
4		work	
5	ToMM dinner prep		work
6	dinner	dinner	dinner
7	family time	family time	family time
8			
9			
10			
11			
12	sleep	sleep	sleep

THURSDAY	FRIDAY	SATURDAY	SUNDAY
get ready	get ready		
breakfast	breakfast		
school run	ToMM life admin		
work	work		
lunch	lunch	HOW I ROLL
work	work	ON A WEEKDAY
school run	work	(TERM TIME)
ToMM dinner prep			
dinner	dinner		
family time	family time		
sleep	sleep		

THE FUN PART

Now comes the fun part! Your Level 3s can be whatever you want them to be; they are there to serve your every whim and fancy. Each week you can focus on how you want to use them. Do you want to have a movie night as the nights draw in or will you plan a picnic in the park with your friends (fizz optional, but encouraged)? Want to start that dreamed of side hustle, take up a hobby? Whatever it is, go for it.

Just as the journal in Part Two includes two pages per week for your housework and meal planning, there are also two pages each week dedicated to how you spend your time. The first column will help you plan your Level 2 time in more detail, if you need to, and to schedule any miscellaneous 'to-do' tasks as and when they crop up, such as a trip to the dentist. I like to use this section to help me compartmentalise my work time, as well as noting those miscellaneous to-dos. (Note that an awful lot of our Level 2 stuff stays the same and it would be a waste of time to write in 'take little 'un to school' every day! – that's what your basic time-slot/framework chart is for – so use your to-do column wisely.)

The second column ensures your Level 3 'me' time activities stay at the forefront of your mind. Make sure, however, that you follow the framework/time-slot chart for your Level 1s and 2s as this ensures that you are safeguarding your free time. On pages 32 to 33 you'll see an example of one of my 'My Time' journal entries. It was for a week when we were having glorious weather!

THE IMPORTANCE OF BEING FLUID WITH YOUR BUDGET

Life sometimes likes to throw a spanner in the works so it's important to realise that occasionally we just have to go with the flow. We can be coasting along quite happily when – boom! Everything gets flung into disarray and we are left scrambling to get our days back on track. For this reason, it's important to remember that this isn't a prescriptive plan. We need to move with the push and pull, not only of our lives but also of our days. Things happen and that's OK. Getting stressed about a change of plan will just make it even harder for you to get back on track. To safeguard your time from unexpected events (whether it's a work emergency, a poo-nami or a sick kid), it's a good idea to have a contingency plan. I plan my week in advance on a Sunday, which means I can see all my Level 1s and 2s clearly and which things can be moved around to cover any problem that arises, but I also build in some contingency time. I might slot in a little more time than I think is strictly necessary for a journey or a particular task. Plan in some time buffers to give yourself some wriggle room.

If you want to dive deeper into how you spend your time (maybe you have no idea where all the time goes, maybe you feel like you are not achieving your goals or perhaps you just want to be more productive), then I highly recommend that you read *The Organised Time Technique* and take yourself through a Time Bootcamp, which will help you look at time from a whole new perspective.

MY TIME — WEEK 1

	TO DO	ME TIME
MONDAY	admin/accounts 10–11am consultation 11–12pm creative/content 1–2pm ——— email accountant call with CRMs	walk/podcast 9–10am lunch/book 12–1pm workout 4–5pm evening walk 8–9pm with kids
TUESDAY	consultation 10–11am admin 11–12pm app development 1–2pm creative/content 2–5pm ——— call with developers	walk/podcast 9–10am lunch/ book 12–1pm workout 4–5pm drinks in garden 8–10pm
WEDNESDAY	consultations 10–12pm consultation 1–2pm admin 4–6pm ——— write up consultation emails	yoga 9–10am lunch 12–1pm dinner out 8–10pm with Mike

TO DO	ME TIME	
admin 10–12pm consultations 1–2pm ———————— update blog reply to DMS	walk 9–10am lunch 12–1pm phone sister workout 4–5pm early night 8pm!	THURSDAY
admin 10–12pm creative 1–5pm ———————— pay bills plan future content	workout 9–10am lunch walk 12–1pm nails 5–6pm takeaway night 8pm	FRIDAY
Buy stamps!	THEME PARK	SATURDAY
Online grocery delivery 9am	Sunday lunch at pub 2pm	SUNDAY

HOW TO MAKE THIS JOURNAL WORK FOR YOU

Now that you are up to speed with how TOMM and TOTT work, let's get down to how you can best use the journal in Part Two. You will notice that it is undated. I have chosen to do this because it means you can start using it at any time of the year, have a break and pick it up again and you won't have that annoying expanse of blank pages – they totally ruin the vibe! It can't be just me who *hates this*.

I have woven both TOMM and TOTT into the structure of the journal so that it will act as your mission control, perfectly combining the two methods to make sure that your life runs as smoothly as possible, and that you give yourself as much attention as your house, your work and all the other stuff that needs your consideration. (If you've flicked straight to this section and haven't read my previous books, take a look at the explanations of TOMM and TOTT in the two previous sections so you can get up and running as soon as possible.)

READY FOR A LITTLE BIT OF JOURNAL ORIENTATION?

Each month starts with two opening pages. On the first, write down your ideas for being your future friend (see page 27) this month and any general notes you might want to make. Opposite this is a 'this month' page featuring my inspirational quote for the month and lots of space for you to get creative and decorate or fill in as you wish. Go wild, let your creativity run free (or you can just write in the month if that's your bag!). I would love to see the results of your creativity, so please make sure you snap a picture and tag me in on your socials.

Next you will see two pages dedicated to 'My Home', followed by another two allocated to 'My Time'. Let's look at each of these checklist charts in turn, and how you can use them in a way that's right for you.

'My Home' checklists

These journal pages are your weekly command centre for keeping on top of the household tasks. This is where you will fill in and keep track of your TOMM jobs for the coming week (including the room that will be that week's Focus).

As I mentioned in the introductory section on TOMM, you can adapt my default jobs and mould the method to perfectly fit your home, by completing the blank TOMM Level 2 checklist chart on page 38. As per my checklist on page 14, fill in the tasks that are specific to your home and use that as your guide to what you should be doing in each room on that particular day. Unlike my sample checklist on page 14, this chart doesn't specify the days for each room, so you can decide that for yourself: for example, you may want to do the kitchen on a Monday or make Thursday your Focus Day, rather than Friday. The same applies to the blank Focus Day chart on page 40, so add the rooms and tasks that best fit with your home.

THE 30 MINUTES GOLDEN RULES

Following these rules will ensure that you are as efficient as possible with the 30 minutes you have for your Level 2 and Focus Day tasks.

• **Use a timer** This is non-negotiable. You might find that you severely underestimate, or heavily overestimate, the time that you spend on a certain tasks.

• **Your list of jobs should be specific to your home** Yes, my Level 2 checklist chart on page 14 is great for suggestions, but I don't know how your home functions and I don't know how many people live there. Add or take things away as necessary.

• **Start with the most urgent jobs** Before you set the timer, have a look around the room that you are about to tackle. Make a mental note and have a plan of action.

• **When you are in each room, plan what you need to do for your Focus Day** This way you will know what needs doing, and you can make use of your time as effectively as possible.

T.O.M.M.

MY LEVEL 2
CHECKLIST

T.O.M.M.

MY FOCUS DAY CHECKLIST

Remember: 30 minutes only!

Week 1:

Week 2:

Week 3:

Week 4:

Week 5:

Week 6:

Week 7:

Week 8:

Remember: the Focus Day is the key to TOMM.

Once you have created your own personal version of TOMM in these two charts, they will become your housework reference page for the rest of the journal. Note that I haven't provided a blank chart for Level 1 tasks, as those basic tasks – making the beds, vacuuming, laundry and keeping the bathroom clean – tend to be hardwired into how we go about our day. (Personally, I couldn't get through the day without cleaning the loos and putting on a load of washing!). However, in the journal I've put in an extra blank box so that you can add in any other cleaning task or other chore that you might want to remind yourself to do each day.

When it comes to filling in the charts in the journal, at the start of each week, fill in your Focus room for that week (see page 17 for the running order I follow) and, as you go through the week, tick off your Level 1 daily jobs each day (or if you're not quite such as stickler for detail, just use them as a reminder). Then tick your Level 2s and Focus jobs – your Monday to Friday jobs – as you do them. Until you get the hang of what you need to do in each room, refer to your charts as a reminder.

Part and parcel of getting through the week feeling that everything in your home is under control is, of course, food! After all, you can't clean on an empty stomach. This is why I've provided a page for you to fill in your menu plan and shopping list for the week ahead. I find it really handy to have that in the same place as my housework 'to-do' list – so that I can see what I've got coming up in the kitchen.

'My Time' pages and time schedule diary

The 'My Time' pages in the journal help you to focus on your TOTT plan for the week, encouraging you to stick to your schedule and, just as importantly, keep those 'me' time Level 3s on your radar. Use my examples in the 'TOTT explained' section (see page 23) to help you think about how you want to structure your days, but remember that everyone is different and what works for me might not work for you.

Before you start adding to the 'My Time' pages in the journal, fill in the time schedule diary overleaf and use this as your foundation for how you plan what you are going to fit into your days. Look at your daily units as a blank canvas, and have fun experimenting and creating new routines. By laying out your Level 1 and regular Level 2 time commitments you will be able to see much more clearly how much time you have left for the level Level 3 fun stuff! You can be as detailed as you like; if you need strict timings then go for it, but if you would prefer to be a little more fluid then the chart will accommodate looser timings too. The most important thing is that you stick to your plan so that you have a good balance of work and fun!

One important point: I realise that not everyone's schedule remains the same throughout the year (I'm thinking particularly of those who have school-age children) so you can either fill this in in pencil and alter it accordingly or use the spare time schedule diary (see the very last pages of this book) for those times when your life flows to a different rhythm.

TIME	MONDAY	TUESDAY	WEDNESDAY
6			
7			
8			
9			
10			
11			
12			
1			
2			
3			
4			
5			
6			
7			
8			
9			
10			
11			
12			

THURSDAY	FRIDAY	SATURDAY	SUNDAY

Want more? Towards the back of this book, you will find more sections packed with lots of other invaluable stuff to help you organise your life, including how to get prepared for Christmas.

Pens at the ready? Visualise how amazing this journal will look at the end of a year, all ticked off and complete and, not only that, how amazing will your house look?! What a beautiful accomplishment. Let's get going!

PART TWO

THE JOURNAL

FUTURE FRIEND PROMPTS

NOTES

THIS MONTH

'Do something that your future friend will be thankful for'

MENU PLAN

SHOPPING LIST

MY HOME – WEEK

DAILY JOBS

Beds	Vacuum	Laundry

Bathrooms	

MONDAY TO FRIDAY

Living Room	Bedrooms	Hall and Stairs

Kitchen

Focus this Week

MY TIME – WEEK

	TO DO	ME TIME
MONDAY		
TUESDAY		
WEDNESDAY		

TO DO	ME TIME	
		THURSDAY
		FRIDAY
		SATURDAY
		SUNDAY

MENU PLAN

SHOPPING LIST

MY HOME – WEEK

DAILY JOBS

Beds	Vacuum	Laundry

Bathrooms	

MONDAY TO FRIDAY

Living Room	Bedrooms	Hall and Stairs

Kitchen

Focus this Week

MY TIME – WEEK

	TO DO	ME TIME
MONDAY		
TUESDAY		
WEDNESDAY		

TO DO	ME TIME	
		THURSDAY
		FRIDAY
		SATURDAY
		SUNDAY

MENU PLAN

SHOPPING LIST

MY HOME – WEEK

DAILY JOBS

Beds	Vacuum	Laundry

Bathrooms	

MONDAY TO FRIDAY

Living Room	Bedrooms	Hall and Stairs

Kitchen

Focus this Week

MY TIME – WEEK

	TO DO	ME TIME
MONDAY		
TUESDAY		
WEDNESDAY		

TO DO	ME TIME	
		THURSDAY
		FRIDAY
		SATURDAY
		SUNDAY

MENU PLAN

SHOPPING LIST

MY HOME – WEEK

DAILY JOBS

Beds	Vacuum	Laundry

Bathrooms	

MONDAY TO FRIDAY

Living Room	Bedrooms	Hall and Stairs

Kitchen

Focus this Week

MY TIME – WEEK

	TO DO	ME TIME
MONDAY		
TUESDAY		
WEDNESDAY		

TO DO	ME TIME	
		THURSDAY
		FRIDAY
		SATURDAY
		SUNDAY

FUTURE FRIEND PROMPTS

NOTES

THIS MONTH

'Remember there is no such thing as perfect.
Good enough is good enough'

MENU PLAN

SHOPPING LIST

MY HOME – WEEK

DAILY JOBS

Beds	Vacuum	Laundry

Bathrooms	

MONDAY TO FRIDAY

Living Room	Bedrooms	Hall and Stairs

Kitchen

Focus this Week

MY TIME – WEEK

	TO DO	ME TIME
MONDAY		
TUESDAY		
WEDNESDAY		

	TO DO	ME TIME	
THURSDAY			
FRIDAY			
SATURDAY			
SUNDAY			

MENU PLAN

SHOPPING LIST

MY HOME – WEEK

DAILY JOBS

Beds	Vacuum	Laundry

Bathrooms	

MONDAY TO FRIDAY

Living Room	Bedrooms	Hall and Stairs

Kitchen

Focus this Week

MY TIME — WEEK

	TO DO	ME TIME
MONDAY		
TUESDAY		
WEDNESDAY		

TO DO

ME TIME

THURSDAY

FRIDAY

SATURDAY

SUNDAY

MENU PLAN

SHOPPING LIST

MY HOME — WEEK

DAILY JOBS

Beds	Vacuum	Laundry

Bathrooms	

MONDAY TO FRIDAY

Living Room	Bedrooms	Hall and Stairs

Kitchen

Focus this Week

MY TIME — WEEK

	TO DO	ME TIME
MONDAY		
TUESDAY		
WEDNESDAY		

	TO DO	ME TIME	
THURSDAY			
FRIDAY			
SATURDAY			
SUNDAY			

MENU PLAN

SHOPPING LIST

MY HOME – WEEK

DAILY JOBS

Beds	Vacuum	Laundry

Bathrooms	

MONDAY TO FRIDAY

Living Room	Bedrooms	Hall and Stairs

Kitchen

Focus this Week

MY TIME – WEEK

	TO DO	ME TIME
MONDAY		
TUESDAY		
WEDNESDAY		

TO DO	ME TIME	
		THURSDAY
		FRIDAY
		SATURDAY
		SUNDAY

FUTURE FRIEND PROMPTS

NOTES

THIS MONTH

'Aim for progress, not perfection'

MENU PLAN

SHOPPING LIST

MY HOME — WEEK

DAILY JOBS

Beds	Vacuum	Laundry

Bathrooms	

MONDAY TO FRIDAY

Living Room	Bedrooms	Hall and Stairs

Kitchen

Focus this Week

MY TIME — WEEK

	TO DO	ME TIME
MONDAY		
TUESDAY		
WEDNESDAY		

TO DO	ME TIME	
		THURSDAY
		FRIDAY
		SATURDAY
		SUNDAY

MENU PLAN

SHOPPING LIST

MY HOME – WEEK

DAILY JOBS

Beds	Vacuum	Laundry

Bathrooms	

MONDAY TO FRIDAY

Living Room	Bedrooms	Hall and Stairs

Kitchen

Focus this Week

MY TIME — WEEK

	TO DO	ME TIME
MONDAY		
TUESDAY		
WEDNESDAY		

TO DO	ME TIME	
		THURSDAY
		FRIDAY
		SATURDAY
		SUNDAY

MENU PLAN

SHOPPING LIST

MY HOME – WEEK

DAILY JOBS

Beds	Vacuum	Laundry

Bathrooms	

MONDAY TO FRIDAY

Living Room	Bedrooms	Hall and Stairs

Kitchen

Focus this Week

MY TIME – WEEK

	TO DO	ME TIME
MONDAY		
TUESDAY		
WEDNESDAY		

	TO DO	ME TIME	
			THURSDAY
			FRIDAY
			SATURDAY
			SUNDAY

MENU PLAN

SHOPPING LIST

MY HOME — WEEK

DAILY JOBS

Beds	Vacuum	Laundry

Bathrooms	

MONDAY TO FRIDAY

Living Room	Bedrooms	Hall and Stairs

Kitchen

Focus this Week

MY TIME – WEEK

	TO DO	ME TIME
MONDAY		
TUESDAY		
WEDNESDAY		

TO DO	ME TIME	
		THURSDAY
		FRIDAY
		SATURDAY
		SUNDAY

FUTURE FRIEND PROMPTS

NOTES

THIS MONTH

'If you feel you've got too much on,
ask yourself the killer question,
"What would happen if I don't do it?"
It will help you to prioritise'

MENU PLAN

SHOPPING LIST

MY HOME – WEEK

DAILY JOBS

Beds	Vacuum	Laundry

Bathrooms	

MONDAY TO FRIDAY

Living Room	Bedrooms	Hall and Stairs

Kitchen

Focus this Week

MY TIME — WEEK

	TO DO	ME TIME
MONDAY		
TUESDAY		
WEDNESDAY		

	TO DO	ME TIME
THURSDAY		
FRIDAY		
SATURDAY		
SUNDAY		

MENU PLAN

SHOPPING LIST

MY HOME – WEEK

DAILY JOBS

Beds	Vacuum	Laundry

Bathrooms	

MONDAY TO FRIDAY

Living Room	Bedrooms	Hall and Stairs

Kitchen

Focus this Week

MY TIME – WEEK

	TO DO	ME TIME
MONDAY		
TUESDAY		
WEDNESDAY		

TO DO	ME TIME	
		THURSDAY
		FRIDAY
		SATURDAY
		SUNDAY

MENU PLAN

SHOPPING LIST

MY HOME – WEEK

DAILY JOBS

Beds	Vacuum	Laundry

Bathrooms	

MONDAY TO FRIDAY

Living Room	Bedrooms	Hall and Stairs

Kitchen

Focus this Week

MY TIME – WEEK

	TO DO	ME TIME
MONDAY		
TUESDAY		
WEDNESDAY		

TO DO	ME TIME	
		THURSDAY
		FRIDAY
		SATURDAY
		SUNDAY

MENU PLAN

SHOPPING LIST

MY HOME – WEEK

DAILY JOBS

Beds	Vacuum	Laundry

Bathrooms	

MONDAY TO FRIDAY

Living Room	Bedrooms	Hall and Stairs

Kitchen

Focus this Week

MY TIME – WEEK

	TO DO	ME TIME
MONDAY		
TUESDAY		
WEDNESDAY		

TO DO	ME TIME	
		THURSDAY
		FRIDAY
		SATURDAY
		SUNDAY

FUTURE FRIEND PROMPTS

NOTES

THIS MONTH

'Do your TOMM jobs and then go and do something fun, because there is more to life than housework'

MENU PLAN

SHOPPING LIST

MY HOME — WEEK

DAILY JOBS

Beds	Vacuum	Laundry

Bathrooms	

MONDAY TO FRIDAY

Living Room	Bedrooms	Hall and Stairs

Kitchen

Focus this Week

MY TIME — WEEK

	TO DO	ME TIME
MONDAY		
TUESDAY		
WEDNESDAY		

TO DO	ME TIME	
		THURSDAY
		FRIDAY
		SATURDAY
		SUNDAY

MENU PLAN

SHOPPING LIST

MY HOME – WEEK

DAILY JOBS

Beds	Vacuum	Laundry

Bathrooms	

MONDAY TO FRIDAY

Living Room	Bedrooms	Hall and Stairs

Kitchen

Focus this Week

MY TIME — WEEK

	TO DO	ME TIME
MONDAY		
TUESDAY		
WEDNESDAY		

TO DO	ME TIME	
		THURSDAY
		FRIDAY
		SATURDAY
		SUNDAY

MENU PLAN

SHOPPING LIST

MY HOME – WEEK

DAILY JOBS

Beds	Vacuum	Laundry

Bathrooms	

MONDAY TO FRIDAY

Living Room	Bedrooms	Hall and Stairs

Kitchen

Focus this Week

MY TIME – WEEK

	TO DO	ME TIME
MONDAY		
TUESDAY		
WEDNESDAY		

TO DO

ME TIME

THURSDAY

FRIDAY

SATURDAY

SUNDAY

MENU PLAN

SHOPPING LIST

MY HOME — WEEK

DAILY JOBS

Beds	Vacuum	Laundry

Bathrooms	

MONDAY TO FRIDAY

Living Room	Bedrooms	Hall and Stairs

Kitchen

Focus this Week

MY TIME — WEEK

	TO DO	ME TIME
MONDAY		
TUESDAY		
WEDNESDAY		

TO DO	ME TIME	
		THURSDAY
		FRIDAY
		SATURDAY
		SUNDAY

FUTURE FRIEND PROMPTS

NOTES

THIS MONTH

'Little by little, day by day, as long as you do something to move towards your goals, you are winning'

MENU PLAN

SHOPPING LIST

MY HOME – WEEK

DAILY JOBS

Beds	Vacuum	Laundry

Bathrooms	

MONDAY TO FRIDAY

Living Room	Bedrooms	Hall and Stairs

Kitchen

Focus this Week

MY TIME — WEEK

	TO DO	ME TIME
MONDAY		
TUESDAY		
WEDNESDAY		

	TO DO	ME TIME	
			THURSDAY
			FRIDAY
			SATURDAY
			SUNDAY

MENU PLAN

SHOPPING LIST

MY HOME – WEEK

DAILY JOBS

Beds	Vacuum	Laundry

Bathrooms	

MONDAY TO FRIDAY

Living Room	Bedrooms	Hall and Stairs

Kitchen

Focus this Week

MY TIME – WEEK

	TO DO	ME TIME
MONDAY		
TUESDAY		
WEDNESDAY		

TO DO	ME TIME	
		THURSDAY
		FRIDAY
		SATURDAY
		SUNDAY

MENU PLAN

SHOPPING LIST

MY HOME – WEEK

DAILY JOBS

Beds	Vacuum	Laundry

Bathrooms	

MONDAY TO FRIDAY

Living Room	Bedrooms	Hall and Stairs

Kitchen

Focus this Week

MY TIME – WEEK

	TO DO	ME TIME
MONDAY		
TUESDAY		
WEDNESDAY		

TO DO	ME TIME	
		THURSDAY
		FRIDAY
		SATURDAY
		SUNDAY

MENU PLAN

SHOPPING LIST

MY HOME – WEEK

DAILY JOBS

Beds	Vacuum	Laundry

Bathrooms	

MONDAY TO FRIDAY

Living Room	Bedrooms	Hall and Stairs

Kitchen

Focus this Week

MY TIME – WEEK

	TO DO	ME TIME
MONDAY		
TUESDAY		
WEDNESDAY		

TO DO	ME TIME	
		THURSDAY
		FRIDAY
		SATURDAY
		SUNDAY

FUTURE FRIEND PROMPTS

NOTES

THIS MONTH

'Think about this: there are 1440 minutes in every day. What are you going to do with yours?'

MENU PLAN

SHOPPING LIST

MY HOME – WEEK

DAILY JOBS

Beds	Vacuum	Laundry

Bathrooms	

MONDAY TO FRIDAY

Living Room	Bedrooms	Hall and Stairs

Kitchen

Focus this Week

MY TIME — WEEK

	TO DO	ME TIME
MONDAY		
TUESDAY		
WEDNESDAY		

TO DO	ME TIME	
		THURSDAY
		FRIDAY
		SATURDAY
		SUNDAY

MENU PLAN

SHOPPING LIST

MY HOME – WEEK

DAILY JOBS

Beds	Vacuum	Laundry

Bathrooms	

MONDAY TO FRIDAY

Living Room	Bedrooms	Hall and Stairs

Kitchen

Focus this Week

MY TIME – WEEK

	TO DO	ME TIME
MONDAY		
TUESDAY		
WEDNESDAY		

TO DO	ME TIME	
		THURSDAY
		FRIDAY
		SATURDAY
		SUNDAY

MENU PLAN

SHOPPING LIST

MY HOME — WEEK

DAILY JOBS

Beds	Vacuum	Laundry

Bathrooms	

MONDAY TO FRIDAY

Living Room	Bedrooms	Hall and Stairs

Kitchen

Focus this Week

MY TIME — WEEK

	TO DO	ME TIME
MONDAY		
TUESDAY		
WEDNESDAY		

TO DO

ME TIME

THURSDAY

FRIDAY

SATURDAY

SUNDAY

MENU PLAN

SHOPPING LIST

MY HOME – WEEK

DAILY JOBS

Beds	Vacuum	Laundry

Bathrooms	

MONDAY TO FRIDAY

Living Room	Bedrooms	Hall and Stairs

Kitchen

Focus this Week

MY TIME – WEEK

	TO DO	ME TIME
MONDAY		
TUESDAY		
WEDNESDAY		

TO DO	ME TIME	
		THURSDAY
		FRIDAY
		SATURDAY
		SUNDAY

FUTURE FRIEND PROMPTS

NOTES

THIS MONTH

'Remember that doing a little bit is much better than doing nothing at all'

MENU PLAN

SHOPPING LIST

MY HOME — WEEK

DAILY JOBS

Beds	Vacuum	Laundry

Bathrooms	

MONDAY TO FRIDAY

Living Room	Bedrooms	Hall and Stairs

Kitchen

Focus this Week

MY TIME - WEEK

	TO DO	ME TIME
MONDAY		
TUESDAY		
WEDNESDAY		

	TO DO	ME TIME	
			THURSDAY
			FRIDAY
			SATURDAY
			SUNDAY

MENU PLAN

SHOPPING LIST

MY HOME – WEEK

DAILY JOBS

Beds	Vacuum	Laundry

Bathrooms	

MONDAY TO FRIDAY

Living Room	Bedrooms	Hall and Stairs

Kitchen

Focus this Week

MY TIME – WEEK

	TO DO	ME TIME
MONDAY		
TUESDAY		
WEDNESDAY		

	TO DO	ME TIME	
			THURSDAY
			FRIDAY
			SATURDAY
			SUNDAY

MENU PLAN

SHOPPING LIST

MY HOME – WEEK

DAILY JOBS

Beds	Vacuum	Laundry

Bathrooms	

MONDAY TO FRIDAY

Living Room	Bedrooms	Hall and Stairs

Kitchen

Focus this Week

MY TIME – WEEK

	TO DO	ME TIME
MONDAY		
TUESDAY		
WEDNESDAY		

TO DO	ME TIME	
		THURSDAY
		FRIDAY
		SATURDAY
		SUNDAY

MENU PLAN

SHOPPING LIST

MY HOME – WEEK

DAILY JOBS

Beds	Vacuum	Laundry

Bathrooms	

MONDAY TO FRIDAY

Living Room	Bedrooms	Hall and Stairs

Kitchen

Focus this Week

MY TIME – WEEK

	TO DO	ME TIME
MONDAY		
TUESDAY		
WEDNESDAY		

	TO DO	ME TIME	
			THURSDAY
			FRIDAY
			SATURDAY
			SUNDAY

FUTURE FRIEND PROMPTS

NOTES

THIS MONTH

'Prioritise what matters'

MENU PLAN

SHOPPING LIST

MY HOME – WEEK

DAILY JOBS

Beds	Vacuum	Laundry

Bathrooms	

MONDAY TO FRIDAY

Living Room	Bedrooms	Hall and Stairs

Kitchen

Focus this Week

MY TIME – WEEK

	TO DO	ME TIME
MONDAY		
TUESDAY		
WEDNESDAY		

	TO DO	ME TIME
THURSDAY		
FRIDAY		
SATURDAY		
SUNDAY		

MENU PLAN

SHOPPING LIST

MY HOME – WEEK

DAILY JOBS

Beds	Vacuum	Laundry

Bathrooms	

MONDAY TO FRIDAY

Living Room	Bedrooms	Hall and Stairs

Kitchen

Focus this Week

MY TIME – WEEK

	TO DO	ME TIME
MONDAY		
TUESDAY		
WEDNESDAY		

TO DO	ME TIME	
		THURSDAY
		FRIDAY
		SATURDAY
		SUNDAY

MENU PLAN

SHOPPING LIST

MY HOME – WEEK

DAILY JOBS

Beds	Vacuum	Laundry

Bathrooms	

MONDAY TO FRIDAY

Living Room	Bedrooms	Hall and Stairs

Kitchen

Focus this Week

MY TIME – WEEK

	TO DO	ME TIME
MONDAY		
TUESDAY		
WEDNESDAY		

TO DO	ME TIME	
		THURSDAY
		FRIDAY
		SATURDAY
		SUNDAY

MENU PLAN

SHOPPING LIST

MY HOME – WEEK

DAILY JOBS

Beds	Vacuum	Laundry

Bathrooms	

MONDAY TO FRIDAY

Living Room	Bedrooms	Hall and Stairs

Kitchen

Focus this Week

MY TIME – WEEK

	TO DO	ME TIME
MONDAY		
TUESDAY		
WEDNESDAY		

TO DO	ME TIME	
		THURSDAY
		FRIDAY
		SATURDAY
		SUNDAY

FUTURE FRIEND PROMPTS

NOTES

THIS MONTH

*'Embrace the fact that relaxing
is not a waste of time'*

MENU PLAN

SHOPPING LIST

MY HOME – WEEK

DAILY JOBS

Beds	Vacuum	Laundry

Bathrooms	

MONDAY TO FRIDAY

Living Room	Bedrooms	Hall and Stairs

Kitchen

Focus this Week

MY TIME — WEEK

	TO DO	ME TIME
MONDAY		
TUESDAY		
WEDNESDAY		

	TO DO	ME TIME	
			THURSDAY
			FRIDAY
			SATURDAY
			SUNDAY

MENU PLAN

SHOPPING LIST

MY HOME – WEEK

DAILY JOBS

Beds	Vacuum	Laundry

Bathrooms	

MONDAY TO FRIDAY

Living Room	Bedrooms	Hall and Stairs

Kitchen

Focus this Week

MY TIME — WEEK

	TO DO	ME TIME
MONDAY		
TUESDAY		
WEDNESDAY		

	TO DO	ME TIME	
THURSDAY			
FRIDAY			
SATURDAY			
SUNDAY			

MENU PLAN

SHOPPING LIST

MY HOME – WEEK

DAILY JOBS

Beds	Vacuum	Laundry

Bathrooms	

MONDAY TO FRIDAY

Living Room	Bedrooms	Hall and Stairs

Kitchen

Focus this Week

MY TIME – WEEK

	TO DO	ME TIME
MONDAY		
TUESDAY		
WEDNESDAY		

TO DO	ME TIME	
		THURSDAY
		FRIDAY
		SATURDAY
		SUNDAY

MENU PLAN

SHOPPING LIST

MY HOME – WEEK

DAILY JOBS

Beds	Vacuum	Laundry

Bathrooms	

MONDAY TO FRIDAY

Living Room	Bedrooms	Hall and Stairs

Kitchen

Focus this Week

MY TIME — WEEK

	TO DO	ME TIME
MONDAY		
TUESDAY		
WEDNESDAY		

	TO DO	ME TIME	
			THURSDAY
			FRIDAY
			SATURDAY
			SUNDAY

FUTURE FRIEND PROMPTS

NOTES

THIS MONTH

'If you are sick of starting again, stop throwing in the towel'

MENU PLAN

SHOPPING LIST

MY HOME – WEEK

DAILY JOBS

Beds	Vacuum	Laundry

Bathrooms	

MONDAY TO FRIDAY

Living Room	Bedrooms	Hall and Stairs

Kitchen

Focus this Week

MY TIME — WEEK

	TO DO	ME TIME
MONDAY		
TUESDAY		
WEDNESDAY		

TO DO	ME TIME	
		THURSDAY
		FRIDAY
		SATURDAY
		SUNDAY

MENU PLAN

SHOPPING LIST

MY HOME — WEEK

DAILY JOBS

Beds	Vacuum	Laundry

Bathrooms	

MONDAY TO FRIDAY

Living Room	Bedrooms	Hall and Stairs

Kitchen

Focus this Week

MY TIME — WEEK

	TO DO	ME TIME
MONDAY		
TUESDAY		
WEDNESDAY		

	TO DO	ME TIME	
THURSDAY			
FRIDAY			
SATURDAY			
SUNDAY			

MENU PLAN

SHOPPING LIST

MY HOME – WEEK

DAILY JOBS

Beds	Vacuum	Laundry

Bathrooms	

MONDAY TO FRIDAY

Living Room	Bedrooms	Hall and Stairs

Kitchen

Focus this Week

MY TIME – WEEK

	TO DO	ME TIME
MONDAY		
TUESDAY		
WEDNESDAY		

TO DO	ME TIME	
		THURSDAY
		FRIDAY
		SATURDAY
		SUNDAY

MENU PLAN

SHOPPING LIST

MY HOME – WEEK

DAILY JOBS

Beds	Vacuum	Laundry

Bathrooms	

MONDAY TO FRIDAY

Living Room	Bedrooms	Hall and Stairs

Kitchen

Focus this Week

MY TIME – WEEK

	TO DO	ME TIME
MONDAY		
TUESDAY		
WEDNESDAY		

TO DO	ME TIME	
		THURSDAY
		FRIDAY
		SATURDAY
		SUNDAY

FUTURE FRIEND PROMPTS

NOTES

THIS MONTH

'Be persistent. Be consistent'

MENU PLAN

SHOPPING LIST

MY HOME – WEEK

DAILY JOBS

Beds	Vacuum	Laundry

Bathrooms	

MONDAY TO FRIDAY

Living Room	Bedrooms	Hall and Stairs

Kitchen

Focus this Week

MY TIME – WEEK

	TO DO	ME TIME
MONDAY		
TUESDAY		
WEDNESDAY		

TO DO	ME TIME	
		THURSDAY
		FRIDAY
		SATURDAY
		SUNDAY

MENU PLAN

SHOPPING LIST

MY HOME — WEEK

DAILY JOBS

Beds	Vacuum	Laundry

Bathrooms	

MONDAY TO FRIDAY

Living Room	Bedrooms	Hall and Stairs

Kitchen

Focus this Week

MY TIME – WEEK

	TO DO	ME TIME
MONDAY		
TUESDAY		
WEDNESDAY		

TO DO	ME TIME	
		THURSDAY
		FRIDAY
		SATURDAY
		SUNDAY

MENU PLAN

SHOPPING LIST

MY HOME – WEEK

DAILY JOBS

Beds	Vacuum	Laundry

Bathrooms	

MONDAY TO FRIDAY

Living Room	Bedrooms	Hall and Stairs

Kitchen

Focus this Week

MY TIME – WEEK

	TO DO	ME TIME
MONDAY		
TUESDAY		
WEDNESDAY		

TO DO	ME TIME	
		THURSDAY
		FRIDAY
		SATURDAY
		SUNDAY

MENU PLAN

SHOPPING LIST

MY HOME — WEEK

DAILY JOBS

Beds	Vacuum	Laundry

Bathrooms	

MONDAY TO FRIDAY

Living Room	Bedrooms	Hall and Stairs

Kitchen

Focus this Week

MY TIME – WEEK

	TO DO	ME TIME
MONDAY		
TUESDAY		
WEDNESDAY		

	TO DO	ME TIME	
			THURSDAY
			FRIDAY
			SATURDAY
			SUNDAY

PART THREE

THE CLUTTER BUSTER AND THE MESSY HOUSE BOOTCAMP

This section is for you if you feel that the housework has been on the backburner and you need to reset before you can really get started with your TOMM routine.

There is more to life than housework, so when life throws us a curve ball it stands to reason that cleaning might fall to the bottom of the list. Maybe you are recovering from an illness, have recently returned to work, just moved into your first home, or have become a parent for the first time. Perhaps you've simply got out of a routine and it's all become a bit chaotic. Whatever has brought you to the point where you feel you can't see the wood for the trees (or the surfaces for the clutter!) you should never feel guilty about it. As parents, the guilt often comes at us from all sorts of angles. Worrying about a messy living room should not be one of those sources of guilt.

Let's look at how you can move forward. The quick quiz opposite will help you find the best option to begin to tackle the overwhelm. Of course, you might feel that you need to do The Clutter Buster *and* The Messy House Bootcamp. If this applies to you, my advice is to start with The Clutter Buster.

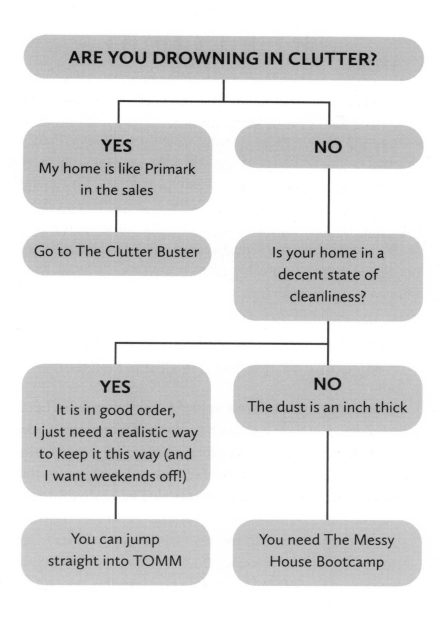

ARE YOU DROWNING IN CLUTTER?

YES
My home is like Primark
in the sales

NO

Go to The Clutter Buster

Is your home in a
decent state of
cleanliness?

YES
It is in good order,
I just need a realistic way
to keep it this way (and
I want weekends off!)

NO
The dust is an inch thick

You can jump
straight into TOMM

You need The Messy
House Bootcamp

THE CLUTTER BUSTER

You can't clean clutter. It really is as simple as that. The Clutter Buster is less about cleaning and more about clearing excess stuff. You will be wasting your time trying to battle through your 30 minutes of TOMM if you are spending most of it picking up stuff that isn't where it belongs. This is the reason for The Clutter Buster. I know that it can seem frustrating – a bit like being kept behind after class – when you simply want to get stuck into keeping on top of everything, but if you have too much stuff it must be dealt with first. Otherwise, you will feel as though you're engaged in a never-ending battle with your home.

My golden rules for The Clutter Buster

• **Know your exits before you begin** Let me explain. Let's pretend that you have a clogged-up loft. You know that you need to clear it out, because when you free up the space in the loft you can then move some of your belongings into the newly cleared attic, freeing up your living space downstairs. But if you don't know how you are going to get rid of the stuff – your exit plan – then you are essentially moving clutter from one place to another. If you don't have a plan, then when you climb down that loft ladder you'll start spinning around in circles on the landing, not knowing what to do with the all the stuff. And bagging it all up and sticking it in the boot of your car just to drive around with it for the next 6 months is no good either.

• **Don't overwhelm yourself** Always tackle small sections at a time; this way you will see all those small chunks of progress start to add up, which will help you stay motivated. Start small (you can always do more if you have the time); even one cupboard or one shelf of a bookcase will help you work towards your goal.

TIPS FOR DECLUTTERING YOUR WARDROBE

Most of us have too many clothes. Here are my tips for tackling the clothing conundrum!

• At the turn of the season pack away anything that you won't be wearing – don't let thick jumpers take up valuable space when it's hot outside; ditto summer dresses and shorts in winter.

• When you pack away your clothes, use it as an opportunity to say goodbye to things that have seen better days, that you haven't worn for ages or that no longer fit.

• Only buy clothes that fit. Obvious you might think but, hang on, don't we all have at least pair of jeans or similar that we think we'll squeeze into one day. Who needs the pressure!

• Buy clothes that suit your lifestyle not your dream lifestyle. I'm a mum of three boys and I work from home. Dry-clean-only dresses and smart office wear simply won't get worn.

THE CLUTTER BUSTER

(No timer needed for this.)

The amount of time that this is going to take will depend on these things:

1. The size of your home.
2. The amount of rooms that need your help.
3. The amount of time you have free.
4. The amount of clutter you have.

If you are lacking in motivation, head over to The Organised Mum Community (see page 314) and we can collectively keep you motivated/kick your butt (whichever you prefer).

Don't forget – before you start

- **Be realistic** You can only keep the amount of stuff you are able to store, so unless you are willing to pay for storage, you are going to have to prepare yourself for some serious culling.
- **Plan the exit route** Remember what I said on the previous page: think about what you are going to do with the stuff. You don't want to end up in a situation where you have piles of rubbish sitting outside in the back garden with no way to get it shifted.

- **Don't start what you can't finish** Make sure you have enough time to complete the tasks you have chosen to do, or you will become demotivated and despondent.

3, 2, 1 – go!

Pick a room

(only do one room at a time)

Sort the clutter into 3 piles:
1 Bin it
2 Keep it
3 Donate it

Take before-and-after pictures to keep you motivated.
Keep going!

Start in the left-hand corner of your room and work your way around clockwise. Have a one-touch policy: if you pick it up, sort it into a pile.

Top tips

- Most councils have a disposal service for bulky items such as fridges and sofas.
- If you are up to your neck in rubbish, it might be worth hiring a skip.
- If you are overly sentimental and are still clinging on to the champagne cork from New Year's Eve 1996, you might need to reassess your emotional connection to inanimate objects.
- Another word about clothes: if you haven't worn it for twelve months, let it go.

THE MESSY HOUSE BOOTCAMP

If you who don't have any clutter but need to fire up the duster again, The Messy House Bootcamp is for you.

We all need a housework reset from time to time. Look upon this as a spring clean that can be done at any time of year. Once you have made your way through The Messy House Bootcamp, you will be able to move to maintenance mode and use TOMM to keep on top of your housework going forward.

Just as with The Clutter Buster there are some golden rules that will make your bootcamp journey so much easier. The bootcamp is not for the faint of heart, but I promise that the end results will be worth it.

My golden rules for The Messy House Bootcamp

• **Take as long as you need** This is my top tip to help you push through the pain. It doesn't need to all get done in the same week, so spread it out over a few weeks if you want to – the most important thing is that you finish what you start.

There is no timer for the Bootcamp, so just as you would if you were following The Clutter Buster, work to the energy and time that you have available. There is nothing worse than starting to Bootcamp your kitchen and, full of great intentions, empty all the cupboards to clean the insides just to run out of steam 30 minutes later. Don't bite off more than you can chew, which brings me on to my next tip.

• **Don't tackle it alone** Get your partner and/or kids involved. I'm willing to bet it isn't just your mess that needs sorting. It will get done much quicker if you divide the tasks and everyone does their bit.

On page 274 you will find The Messy House Bootcamp. Work your way through the tick lists towards a sparkling clean home.

BE KIND TO YOURSELF

Boot-camping your home is not only physically tiring, it can also be emotionally draining. I have worked with lots of families over the years and more often than not a home that needs a housework reset has ended up that way as a consequence of something else that demands a lot of time. This is usually a life event such as having a baby, starting a new job, illness, or spending time caring for others. If you are in this sort of situation and this is your reason for needing to Bootcamp, then please be kind to yourself. Your home didn't get this way overnight and you won't be able to fix it overnight either. Take your time, remember to take breaks, and reward yourself along the way.

THE MESSY HOUSE BOOTCAMP

Monday: living room

- [ ] Declutter
- [ ] Clean the windows and mirrors
- [ ] Wash throws and pet bedding
- [ ] Dust everything
- [ ] Clean the skirting boards
- [ ] Vacuum under the sofa cushions
- [ ] Vacuum under the furniture
- [ ] Mop if applicable

Tuesday: bedrooms

- [ ] Declutter
- [ ] Have a beauty product/ toy cull
- [ ] Clean the windows and mirrors
- [ ] Vacuum and flip the mattresses
- [ ] Dust everything
- [ ] Clean the skirting boards
- [ ] Vacuum
- [ ] Change the bedding

Wednesday: hall and stairs

- [ ] Declutter
- [ ] Have a coat and shoes cull
- [ ] Clean the windows and mirrors
- [ ] Dust everything
- [ ] Clean the banisters and skirting boards
- [ ] Vacuum under the furniture

Thursday: kitchen

- [ ] Empty the crumbs from the toaster
- [ ] Clean out the cutlery drawer(s)
- [ ] Clean out the fridge
- [ ] Dust the blinds
- [ ] Clean the windows
- [ ] Clean the microwave
- [ ] Clean down the tiles
- [ ] Clean the oven and hob
- [ ] Clean all the worktops
- [ ] Clean the cupboard fronts
- [ ] Clean the kickboards
- [ ] Vacuum and mop

Friday: bathrooms

- [ ] Dust the extractor fan
- [ ] Clean out the cabinets
- [ ] Clean the shower curtain/give the shower screen a good scrub
- [ ] Clean the wall tiles
- [ ] Clean the windows and mirrors
- [ ] Scrub the toilet, shower, bath and sink
- [ ] Clean the floor, paying particular attention to the floor around the loo
- [ ] Wash the bathmat

PART FOUR

ORGANISED CHRISTMAS

Ah, Christmas. My absolute favourite time of year (mainly for the food!), but the mince pies and the mulled wine don't taste as good if you are stressed up to the eyeballs, desperately trying to find a Santa that isn't booked up. That's where this part of the journal comes in. We are sorting out the rest of life, so why not get December sorted too?

When I first became a mum, I had no idea about the amount of additional stuff that had to be done at Christmas. Looking back, it probably shouldn't have come as such of a shock. Christmas culture is *very* geared towards children. That first Christmas came like a thunderbolt, and I was so consumed with the idea of making it perfect that I lost sight of actually enjoying it.

The second year, I approached the festivities somewhat differently, making sure that I had all my ducks in a row well in advance, so that I could relish the build-up to Christmas. I came up with a plan, lovingly named Organised Christmas, and it has been my annual saviour ever since. All these years later there are thousands of people following along too. I get thank-you messages every year from people who have had one of their most relaxing Christmases ever and that's how I want you to feel. I want you to enjoy December. I don't want you sitting at your little one's nativity play with one eye on your Amazon basket, panic buying last-minute gifts.

YOU IN? HERE'S HOW IT WORKS

The Organised Christmas is a 13-week plan that will take you up to the start of December. By that point, you will have Christmas all wrapped up (pun intended) so you can sit back and enjoy the build-up to the big day.

It will probably feel a bit weird starting your Christmas prep in September. But heed my warning. Every single year, without fail, people message me telling me that when they saw me starting Christmas preparation in September that they thought it was too early (I get it, some people are still basking in the Med on their sun loungers when week one rolls around). But time rolls on. Summer turns into autumn, autumn turns into winter and before you know it you are minding your own business in Sainsbury's, when you hear the opening bars of The Pogues and Kirsty McColl and the dread sets in. Every year more people message to tell me that they will join in next time, because they feel stressed and are not having a cool Yule.

The Organised Christmas Countdown gives you small manageable jobs to do each week, so don't worry – you won't feel overwhelmed by massive lists. It encourages you to start thinking about everything from your Christmas menu to how much you are going to budget for presents. Oh, and planning in some fun for you too!

Start by working out when Week 1 needs to start. This will be exactly 13 weeks from 1 December. I always like to start it on a Monday. Best get cracking then . . .

Week 1

☐ **Get important Christmas events in the diary**
If you have young children in primary school, try to find out when the nativity play or any other Christmas events are happening. This way, anyone who wants to come along can make sure they book the time off work well in advance.

☐ **Start thinking about food**
I have an online delivery saver with my supermarket. This gives me a priority Christmas delivery slot, which plays a big part in cutting down the stresstive part of Christmas for me. I don't want to be roaming the aisles fighting for my turkey or sprout tree; I want to be drinking mulled wine while the very nice people deliver it all to my door. If you feel the same about supermarkets in December, sign up this week. Check the small print and see if your supermarket gives you a priority slot.

☐ **Book your tickets to see The Big Dude in the red suit**
The popular events sell out *fast*. If the event you want hasn't got tickets on sale yet, find out when they are due to be released and get it in the diary.

☐ **Book new events**
If you want to do more Christmassy events this year, research them and get them in the diary. This will help you to spread the cost, and you will make sure that you won't miss out on tickets for the popular events. Do you always say you'll go to

a pantomime or go ice skating, but you never get round to it? This is your year.

Week 2

☐ Have a toys and clothes clear out

Do it now before everything starts to get crazy busy. Your kids will be back at school and the chances are that you will have accumulated some junk piles over the summer holidays. Now is the time to battle the clutter (don't forget about The Clutter Buster on page 270 if you need some extra motivation). Let's face it, there will be an influx of new stuff coming your way soon. Get ruthless: either donate, bin or list it on selling sites.

☐ Book tickets for travel

If you know that you will be travelling to see family or friends via train this year, book your tickets as early as you can, and if you need to book hotel rooms, do that now, too. They will be so much cheaper and there will be better availability.

If you are spending time away from home, make sure you book the kennels or cat sitters now. They get booked up quickly, so you don't want to be left in a spot with no one to look after Rover and Tiddles.

☐ Send out save-the-date messages

If you want to plan a festive get-together with friends, pick the date this week and send out save-the-date messages to everyone. People get booked up fast at this time of the year (there are only so many weekends in December). Get in there early to make sure that people can make it. If you need to book babysitters, get that booked in too this week if possible.

Week 3

☐ **Have a freezer clear-out**

Is there a lonely box of frozen mince pies lurking from Christmas last year? Get rid of any suspicious-looking packages that are no longer labelled, and try to use up as much food as you can, so that you don't waste anything. Any money that you save on your food bill while you are eating up the contents of your freezer can be put towards your Christmas budget. If necessary, give your freezer a defrost. An empty freezer will give the bakers among us the chance to fill their freezers with lots of festive treats.

☐ **Buy your advent calendar**

If you normally buy your advent calendar from the supermarket in a panic on 30 November, now is your chance to get one step ahead of the game and treat yourself to something a little special. There are loads of amazing advent calendars around now, from beauty ones to Lego ones, but they usually go on sale quite early, and the best ones always sell out fast. Have a little scout around this week and see if there are any that tickle your fancy.

Week 4

☐ **Set your budget**

This is your main task for this week. Think about everything: food, gifts and travel costs, but also remember to plan for all the little miscellaneous things that can add up to quite a hefty sum (such as additional petrol bills, wrapping paper, cards, stamps and batteries). Your budget can be as detailed as you like, but the most important thing is that it must be realistic. Don't overstretch yourself or you will be in for a miserable start to the New Year. January is bad enough as it is without having to go through the whole month skint.

Make a list of who you will be buying presents for, and set a maximum budget for each person. Once you have made your budget and you are happy with it, stick to it. Over the remaining weeks in the Christmas Countdown buy presents when you have the funds, and wrap them as you go. Remember that your aim is to have it all wrapped up by 1 December.

Week 5

☐ **Check your decorations**

This week's job is to go through all your Christmas decorations and do a stock check. Remember that the sole purpose of this plan is to make sure that you enjoy Christmas, and one of the best bits is getting into the festive spirit by decorating your tree. That romantic image that we all have of Christmas will not be how it goes if all your baubles are smashed. Be your future friend and check it all now.

Week 6

☐ **Think about New Year's Eve – seriously!**
Are you planning to go out this New Year's Eve? If the answer to that is yes, then you need to get it booked in now and also get your babysitter booked in. If you usually spend New Year's Eve with a major fear of missing out, this is your year to make sure that it doesn't happen again.

Week 7

☐ **Get serious about present buying**
If you have not started to get serious about present buying, now is the time. This is especially important if you have a partner (or other family member) who is really hard to buy for. You need to talk to them now about what they want. Speak to the kids and let them know that Father Christmas and his elves have a cut-off date for list amendments. This way you won't be in the awful situation where you've spent all your budget and they then think of something that they really want, which means you have to overload your credit card.

Week 8

☐ **Book personal appointments**
Take time to book in all your appointments this week: hair appointments, eyebrows, nails, and so on. There is nothing worse than phoning up to get yourself looking hot to trot and finding that everything is booked up.

☐ **Don't forget your pets**
Do you have pets that need taking care of? Make sure you stock up on their regular flea treatment, get them booked in at the groomers, and so on.

☐ **Starting some new traditions?**
Put some thought into whether you want to start any new traditions. Now that you are organised, and everything is under control, you might have more energy and headspace to add some extra-special trimmings to your family's festive fun. If you want to do elf-on-the-shelf, start thinking of stuff you can do now with the mischievous imp.

☐ **Book your Christmas and New Year's Eve taxis**
It might seem early but get in there before it's too late.

Week 9

☐ **Write your Christmas cards**
If you send Christmas cards, buy them and write them this week, then put them somewhere safe, ready to post on 1

December. If your children are at school and like to send cards to their classmates, buy these this week and get them to write a handful every now and again. This will stop the kind of mammoth card-writing session where the hand-writing ends up extremely questionable by card number 21 of 30.

☐ **Wrap as you go and check overseas posting deadlines**
Make sure to continue to wrap your presents as you go – and also to make sure that all presents are clearly labelled (or you will forget who they are for). If you are posting abroad, check the last postal dates now and plan what you are going to send and when it needs to be sent by.

Week 10

☐ **'Tis the time to think about your Christmas food (again)**
How you approach your Christmas menu will depend on your own individual preferences. I mark Christmas Eve, Christmas Day and Boxing Day as special eating days. This means that we get extra treats and posher grub than normal. By marking your special food days, it will stop you over-ordering, and it also stops me from overeating into the New Year. Sit down and plan your food, and make sure you keep to budget. I think it is really important to keep it all in perspective and not to let the costs spiral out of control. It is so easy to get caught up in all the marketing hype at Christmas, especially when the glitzy adverts start appearing on the television.

Remember: Christmas dinner is just a Sunday lunch with a few bells and whistles.

If you are ordering a turkey, make sure it fits into your oven. If you are buying a frozen turkey, work out how long it will take to defrost, then mark this on your calendar or set a reminder on your phone.

Week 11

☐ **Do a home spruce-up**
It is time for the pre-Christmas spruce-up and home-check. It is always best to start with a clean slate before the decorations go up. If you follow along with TOMM, this week will be a walk in the park for you. But there are a couple of extra things that I want you to look out for. If you are new to TOMM, this week will see you giving your home a reboot, and for that I suggest using The Messy House Bootcamp.

While you are doing your pre-Christmas home check, here are some handy things for you to have on your radar.

- If you haven't already done so, make sure your tree lights work. Since most fairy lights are LED these days, it can be hard to buy replacement bulbs so you may need to replace the whole set if you don't have some spares.

- Have a decent stockpile of batteries, because there is always that one toy.

- Test your smoke alarms.

- Finally, check through your medicine cabinet, throw out anything that is past its best and restock as necessary. Now is the time to also think about any regular medication that you or your family members take and make sure that you put it in your diary to get any repeat prescriptions in plenty of time.

Week 12

☐ **Check you can cater for your guests**
I don't mean food – I'm sure you've already planned that – I'm talking chairs/glasses/crockery and cutlery (you can hire these if you prefer).

☐ **Buy your Christmas crackers**

☐ **Buy two or three emergency gifts**
Good ones to go for are generic bottles of wine for the grown-ups and gift cards for the kiddies. This will have you covered just in case you find yourself in that awkward situation where someone surprises you with a gift and you haven't bought them one.

☐ **Think about teacher gifts**
– and get them bought and wrapped.

Week 13

☐ **It's time to decorate**
This is the final week of the plan, and this is the best bit. I always decorate my house on the first weekend of December, so that is all there is left to do. Go as crazy or as minimal as you want. Remember: this is your Christmas – there are no rules.

Have a wonderful Christmas; you have worked so hard all year and you deserve to enjoy the season. A word to the wise: because you are prepped so well in advance you need to watch out for the temptation to start buying extra little bits here and there. Stand firm – you're sorted!

SOME SPARE WEEKS

As I explained at the start of this journal, it is undated so that you can pick it up at any time of the year and jump straight in. But, being the practical sort, I have included some spare weeks for you, to help mop up any days or weeks that don't fall neatly into a month. There are 48 weeks in the main journal but 52 weeks in the year so you're gonna need those spares! I've also included one other extra week in case you'd like a trial run before you start the main journal – or maybe try a new way of doing things.

You'll see that I've also included an additional blank time schedule diary at the end, as many of us have different schedules out of term time, so you can use this as your alternative to the one on pages 44 to 45.

MENU PLAN

SHOPPING LIST

MY HOME – WEEK

DAILY JOBS

Beds	Vacuum	Laundry

Bathrooms	

MONDAY TO FRIDAY

Living Room	Bedrooms	Hall and Stairs

Kitchen

Focus this Week

MY TIME – WEEK

	TO DO	ME TIME
MONDAY		
TUESDAY		
WEDNESDAY		

TO DO	ME TIME	
		THURSDAY
		FRIDAY
		SATURDAY
		SUNDAY

MENU PLAN

SHOPPING LIST

MY HOME – WEEK

DAILY JOBS

Beds	Vacuum	Laundry

Bathrooms	

MONDAY TO FRIDAY

Living Room	Bedrooms	Hall and Stairs

Kitchen

Focus this Week

MY TIME – WEEK

	TO DO	ME TIME
MONDAY		
TUESDAY		
WEDNESDAY		

TO DO	ME TIME	
		THURSDAY
		FRIDAY
		SATURDAY
		SUNDAY

MENU PLAN

SHOPPING LIST

MY HOME – WEEK

DAILY JOBS

Beds	Vacuum	Laundry

Bathrooms	

MONDAY TO FRIDAY

Living Room	Bedrooms	Hall and Stairs

Kitchen

Focus this Week

MY TIME — WEEK

	TO DO	ME TIME
MONDAY		
TUESDAY		
WEDNESDAY		

TO DO	ME TIME	
		THURSDAY
		FRIDAY
		SATURDAY
		SUNDAY

MENU PLAN

SHOPPING LIST

MY HOME – WEEK

DAILY JOBS

Beds	Vacuum	Laundry

Bathrooms	

MONDAY TO FRIDAY

Living Room	Bedrooms	Hall and Stairs

Kitchen

Focus this Week

MY TIME – WEEK

	TO DO	ME TIME
MONDAY		
TUESDAY		
WEDNESDAY		

	TO DO	ME TIME	
THURSDAY			
FRIDAY			
SATURDAY			
SUNDAY			

MENU PLAN

SHOPPING LIST

MY HOME – WEEK

DAILY JOBS

Beds	Vacuum	Laundry

Bathrooms	

MONDAY TO FRIDAY

Living Room	Bedrooms	Hall and Stairs

Kitchen

Focus this Week

MY TIME - WEEK

	TO DO	ME TIME
MONDAY		
TUESDAY		
WEDNESDAY		

TO DO	ME TIME	
		THURSDAY
		FRIDAY
		SATURDAY
		SUNDAY

TIME	MONDAY	TUESDAY	WEDNESDAY
6			
7			
8			
9			
10			
11			
12			
1			
2			
3			
4			
5			
6			
7			
8			
9			
10			
11			
12			

THURSDAY	FRIDAY	SATURDAY	SUNDAY

Want to join in with the TeamTomm community online?
Inspiration and motivation are only a few clicks away.

Instagram @the_organised_mum
Facebook @theorganisedmum
YouTube @gemmabray

There is also a daily podcast, search TeamTOMM podcast
wherever you get your podcasts.